Beethoven

Brandon Robshaw and Rochelle Scholar

Published in association with The Basic Skills Agency

Hodder & Stoughton

A MEMBER OF THE HODDER HEADLINE GROUP

Acknowledgements

Cover: Fred van Deelen

Illustrations: Mike Bell

Photos: pp iv, 11, 20 Hulton Getty; p 8 Mary Evans Picture Library

Every effort has been made to trace copyright holders of material reproduced in this book. Any rights not acknowledged will be acknowledged in subsequent printings if notice is given to the publisher.

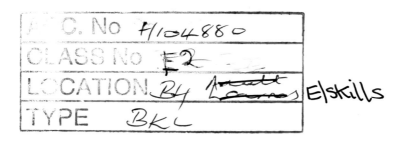
Orders; please contact Bookpoint Ltd, 39 Milton Park, Abingdon, Oxon OX14 4TD. Telephone: (44) 01235 400414, Fax: (44) 01235 400454. Lines are open from 9.00–6.00, Monday to Saturday, with a 24 hour message answering service.
Email address: orders@bookpoint.co.uk

British Library Cataloguing in Publication Data
A catalogue record for this title is available from the British Library

ISBN 0 340 77417 7

First published 2000
Impression number   10 9 8 7 6 5 4 3 2 1
Year   2005 2004 2003 2002 2001 2000

Typeset by Redwood Books Ltd, Trowbridge, Wilts.
Printed in Great Britain for Hodder and Stoughton Educational, a division of Hodder Headline Plc, 338 Euston Road, London NW1 3BH, by Atheneum Press, Gateshead, Tyne & Wear

Contents

1 The Concert

He sat down at the piano.
His name was Ludwig van Beethoven.
He was 25 and the most famous
pianist in Vienna.
He was playing at a private party
for the rich and famous.

The elegant room was full of elegant people.
As they took their seats
they looked over at the pianist.
He sat hunched over the keys.
He was small, stocky and scruffy.
His face was scarred from small pox.
His dark hair stood up wildly.
His dark eyes glittered.

There was a hush.
Beethoven began to play.
The music filled the room.
The audience listened,
silent and still.
They didn't want to miss a note.
It was like nothing they had heard before.
The music seemed to touch the soul.
The music rose and fell.
It became very soft.
And then something very strange happened.
The sound stopped completely.
Beethoven's fingers still ran across the piano keys.
But he was touching them so lightly
that no sound came.
Beethoven did not stop.
He didn't seem to notice that there was no sound.
His face showed that he was still lost in his music.

The audience looked at each other.
What was going on?
Nobody knew what to say.
But the same thought was in everybody's mind.
Could the greatest pianist
in the world
– be deaf?

2 Early Days

Beethoven was 25
when he began to go deaf.
After concerts, he would have a
terrible ringing in his ears.

He didn't want anyone to know.
They wouldn't understand.
How could a composer and performer be deaf?

Beethoven was born in 1770 in Bonn.
His family were poor.
His mother gave birth to seven more
children after Beethoven.

Beethoven's father was a singer at the Court of Bonn.
He did not have much success.
He had a bad temper
and he drank a lot.

He could see that
his son had talent.
Often he would get back late
after a drinking session.
He would drag his young son
out of his bed.
He would make Beethoven practise until dawn.
Beethoven said later that it
made him want to give up.
But his love of music
was already too strong.

Beethoven gave his first concert when he was 7.
His father said he was only 6.
He wanted to make money out of his son's talent.
At school Beethoven looked scruffy.
His mother was ill and couldn't look after the children.

After a time, his father took him out of school.
He thought it best if Beethoven
just worked on his music.
He had piano, organ and violin lessons.

When he was 14,
Beethoven got a job as Court Organist.
The job was quite well paid.
He also gave lessons.

Beethoven's father was drinking heavily.
He was in danger of losing his job.
Beethoven's mother was very weak.
Beethoven had to find another job
which paid more money.
He was the only one able
to look after his family.

By the spring of 1787
he had enough money to go to Vienna.
Vienna was home to the best
composers and the best performers.
Beethoven hoped he could do well there.

3 Vienna

Vienna was like a different world for Ludwig.
It was a city full of life and colour.
There was music everywhere.
People sat in cafes,
drinking and talking.

At this time the most famous
performer in Vienna was Mozart.
Beethoven was very keen to meet Mozart.
He wanted to play for him.
Mozart agreed to meet Beethoven
and to hear him play.

Beethoven sat at the piano and played.
Mozart was not impressed.
'You've just learned that piece off by heart,'
he said. 'Anyone could do that.'

So Beethoven asked Mozart to give
him a tune.
Beethoven improvised on the tune,
adding new bits as he thought of them.

This time Mozart was very impressed.
He turned to the people in the room.
'Keep your eyes on this young man.
Some day he will give the world
something to talk about.'

Mozart

Beethoven smiled.
For the first time in his life
he felt that he could be a great success.

But his trip to Vienna was cut short.
Two weeks later, terrible news reached him.
His mother was dying.
Beethoven had to get back to Bonn.

Beethoven said, 'She was such a kind,
loving mother to me, and my best friend.'
When his mother died the family
had very little money left.
Beethoven's father had spent all his savings
caring for his wife.
He started to drink even more.

Beethoven, at 17, was now head of the family.

4 Deafness Begins

Beethoven went back to playing at the Court.
When famous people came to stay
Beethoven was asked to perform.
One of the guests was
the famous composer, Haydn.

Haydn was very impressed.
He told Ludwig,
'Come back to Vienna with me.
I will help you and be your teacher.'

Beethoven was worried about
leaving his brothers.
However, this was his big chance.

Beethoven had good friends at the Court.
One of his friends told him not to worry.
He got two grants for Beethoven.
The money would help look after his family.

Haydn

Beethoven was 22 when he went back to Vienna.
By the time he was 25
he had became known as a brilliant pianist.
His way of playing was new.
Sometimes it was very loud.
It was always daring and exciting.
The audience said,
'He is not a man, but a devil.'

But his first signs of deafness
were showing.
He wrote to his friend,
'My illness grows worse.
I do not know if I shall ever recover.
I do not want to meet people
because I do not want to say
I am deaf.'

At 32 he decided to give up playing the piano.
He would just compose.
He could hear the music in his head.
In his head, every note was perfect.

5 Beethoven's First Will

One of his friends, Franz, was a doctor.
He said he would try and help Beethoven.
Beethoven told Franz how his ears
buzzed and hummed all day and all night.
He couldn't hear anyone talking quietly.
If people shouted, it was agony for him.

Franz told him to go the country.
He would be able to rest there.
Away from Vienna he would
work on his music.

As the days went by
Beethoven became very depressed.
He felt cut off from the rest of the world.
He wrote a long letter
to his brothers,
to be opened after his death.

He wrote,'I must live alone.
I must live like an outcast.
When I am with people
I'm so afraid that they will
find out I am deaf.'
He wrote, 'People think I have a bad temper.
No one understands.
I could not say, speak louder,
I am deaf.'

Beethoven thought about killing himself.
The letter contained his will.
He left everything to his brothers.

But he did not kill himself.
He decided to go on.
He wrote, 'I will not be crushed by Fate.'
He would live for his music.

He went back to Vienna
and completed his Second Symphony.

6 Unlucky in Love

In the 34 years he lived in Vienna
Beethoven moved 64 times.
Sometimes, he moved to get away from his fans.
Now he was famous
people would hang around
outside his flat.
At other times, he was asked to leave
because he was too noisy,
or because he took
ice cold showers and flooded the floors.

In all these years
he lived alone.
However, he had fallen in love many times.
His friend Franz said,
'There was never a time
when Beethoven wasn't in love.'
He wasn't a good looking man
but there was something about him.
Women found him attractive.

When he was 35 he met two sisters,
Marie-Therese and Josephine.
No one is sure which sister
he fell in love with.
He had close friendships with both women.
His music at this time
was full of his love and passion.

After his death three love letters were found.
They were written to an unknown woman.
The letters have no date on them.
The unknown woman loves Beethoven
but cannot marry him.
No one knows if Beethoven sent these letters.
Maybe they had been returned to him?

7 War in Europe

This was a troubled time in Europe.
Napoleon, the French Leader,
was at war with Austria.

In 1809 his armies
were closing in on Vienna.
Shells and bombs fell on the city.
The noise hurt Beethoven's ears so much,
he had to go down into the cellar
and put pillows over his head.

Beethoven had admired Napoleon.
Beethoven supported the revolution in France.
But Napoleon had crowned himself Emperor.
Beethoven thought this was against
the spirit of the revolution.

When Napoleon was defeated
Beethoven wrote a symphony called 'Battle'.
The money he raised would
go to help wounded soldiers.
It would also help Beethoven clear his debts.

Napoleon

Beethoven conducted the symphony himself.
From the first note he
felt every sound in his body.
As the music fell he fell to his knees.
As the music rose he would reach up high.
He would throw his arms out wide.
But he could not hear the sounds of the orchestra.
And the orchestra could not keep up with Beethoven.
It was nearly a disaster.

Luckily, a second conductor stepped up
onto the stage.
He conducted behind Beethoven.
The orchestra kept their eyes on him.
The symphony was a great success.

Beethoven was nearly totally deaf now.
When he composed on the piano
he had to hold a stick of wood between his teeth.
He would feel the stick tremble
from the notes he played.
This was his only contact with
the music he wrote.

8 Beethoven's Nephew

When Beethoven's brother died
his nephew went to live with him
His nephew was called Karl.
He was nine years old.

As Beethoven had no children,
he wanted to look after Karl.
He didn't like Karl's mother.
He didn't want her to see her son.
Beethoven won a five year court battle
to keep Karl.

He wanted Karl to study music.
He sent him away to school.
But Karl wasn't interested in music.
He wanted to be a soldier when he grew up.

Beethoven and Karl
just couldn't get on.
Beethoven didn't like Karl's friends.
Karl didn't like the way
Beethoven told him what to do all the time.
And he was embarrassed
that his uncle was deaf.
Beethoven's deafness was still getting worse.
He had stopped conducting now.
The last time he tried to conduct,
the theatre manager
sent him a note
in the middle of the concert.
It said, 'I beg you not to go on.'

After reading this Beethoven
stood still for a long time.
With his head bent low
he turned and left the stage.
When he got home
he sat with his head in his hands.

9 The Ninth Symphony

His Ninth Symphony was finished in 1824.
Although Beethoven was ill and worried about Karl
the Ninth Symphony was full of joy.
It was about how the human spirit
can rise above grief.

When the concert took place
there was standing room only.
Beethoven sat with the orchestra.
He couldn't hear a thing.

At the end of the concert,
one of the singers took his hand.
He turned him round.
The audience were clapping and cheering.
Beethoven bowed.
His eyes were full of tears.
When it was all over,
he fainted.

10 'I Shall Hear in Heaven'

Illness, work and worry about Karl
filled Beethoven's mind.
Karl felt that Beethoven
was pushing him too hard.
He went to university but failed his exams.
He wanted to join the army.
Beethoven said he would not allow it.

Karl couldn't take any more.
He bought a shot gun and tried to kill himself.
Luckily, he lived.

He told the police
he had done it because
Beethoven bossed him about too much.

Beethoven loved his nephew very much.
He knew he had to give up
trying to control him.
He agreed that Karl could join the army.

Soon after this, in the winter of 1826,
Beethoven caught pneumonia.
His friends came to see him.
They brought wine and food.
For many years Beethoven
had kept conversation books.
His friends wrote down
what they were talking about for him.

His doctor knew that death was near.
He wrote it down in Beethoven's
conversation book.
Beethoven read the words.
Then he made out his will.
He left all his money to Karl.

On March 24, 1827, he fell into a coma.
Two days later a storm broke out over Vienna.
The sky was black, lit only by the lightning.
Beethoven sat up in the bed.
He stretched his hand out to the sky.
'I shall hear in Heaven,' he said.
Then he fell back.
Dead.

Twenty thousand people
went to his funeral.

Key Dates

December 16, 1779	Ludwig van Beethoven was born in Bonn, Germany
1778	At the age of 8, gives his first public performance
1784	At the age of 14, Beethoven becomes Court Organist
1787	Goes to Vienna, where he meets Mozart. In the same year, his mother dies.
1792	Returns to Vienna and studies with Haydn
1794	Begins to go deaf and starts writing more music, especially for the piano
1799	Writes his First Symphony
1802	Writes his first will and his Second Symphony
1805	Third Symphony
1806	Fourth Symphony
1807	Fifth Symphony
1815	Beethoven adopts his nephew, Karl
1817	Beethoven's deafness is nearly total – he can no longer hear voices
1824	First performance of the Ninth Symphony
1826	Catches pneumonia
March 26, 1827	Beethoven dies